You've Got (Too Much) Mail!

38 Do's and Don'ts to Tame Your Inbox

By Chris A. Baird

If you find this book helpful, please leave a review on Amazon [here][1] . It will help others also find this book.

http://www.powerlists.org/

---

[1] http://www.powerlists.org/9mhm

Table of Contents

1 - Introduction

This book is the third book in the bestselling PowerLists™ book series. Each PowerList™ book is designed to help you get more out of life.

Why Did I Write This Book?

I wrote this book because I know what it's like to be buried in a state of panic under a pile of e-mails. I have discovered several tricks for solving this major problem and I want to set you free from the stress caused by a mountain of e-mails. I also want to show you how it is possible to help other people by changing the way you use e-mail.

How To Use This Book

It is impossible for anyone to implement all of the suggestions I have in this book. However, if my tips help you manage your inbox better and write better e-mails, I will have succeeded in the purpose of this book. Try out the different tips and see what does or doesn't work for you.

You've Got (Too Much) Mail! Cheat Sheet

I created a one page pdf *You've Got (Too Much) Mail! Cheat Sheet*[2] to make it easy for you to be able to follow along as you work through the book. It shows you all 38 Do's and Don'ts and can be used as a checklist or refresher on the different methods explored in the book.

---

[2]http://www.powerlists.org/2vor

2 - Getting Started

What Is E-mail?

E-mails are: "Messages that are sent electronically from one computer to another." - Merriam-Webster

What Is the Problem

This definition doesn't make e-mail sound too stressful. In the past we sent paper letters to each other using a similar system without creating the nightmare that e-mails can cause. It seems the transition shouldn't be such a challenge.

The biggest difference between e-mail and "snail mail" is speed and cost per message. Those two issues alone drive the chaos that e-mail creates. It would be like living in a world in which we were free to drive cars at the speed of light. The number of trips people take would surge. Perhaps your friends would visit you without a break and the number of salespeople at your door would skyrocket.

E-mail has created the problem of too many people trying to communicate with you. It is so cheap and easy to send multiple messages. For these reasons, a serious problem has emerged.

To make things even worse, we ourselves are not innocent. We contribute to piles of e-mails in other people's inboxes. Like pipes in a house that cannot handle the quantity of material being flushed, the toilets overflow.

Are We Ready to Change?

You have two choices:

- Live with this situation of receiving piles of e-mails from others and sending piles of e-mails to others,

OR

- Change how you handle incoming e-mails and how you send e-mails to others.

You are reading this book because you would like to make a change. I am certain you will find some of the strategies to be effective.

3 - Who's the Boss?

"E-mail, instant messaging, and cell phones give us fabulous communication ability, but because we live and work in our own little worlds, that communication is totally disorganized." -- Marilyn vos Savant

What E-mail Should Be

E-mail should be something that saves us time. It makes communication possible with people when they aren't available for meetings. We can communicate with people on the other side of the world.

This means we no longer waste time trying unsuccessfully to call people. In addition, with tighter communication, we can avoid project delays. Instead, we can address issues and resolve them quickly.

What E-mail Isn't

E-mail isn't a means of communicating every thought we have on an issue. It isn't a substitute for actually meeting with people. Some issues can't be resolved through e-mail.

4 - Let's Tame the Beast!

We are now in a great place to go through all the tricks and tips I have discovered for managing e-mails. You will need to decide which tricks work best for you.

(1) Do Unsubscribe to Excessive Newsletter Subscriptions

Receiving newsletters doesn't mean you have the time to read them. If you aren't reading newsletters in your inbox, cancel the subscriptions. It takes time to review your inbox and these newsletters take up valuable time. Make sure that all e-mails you are spending time on are things you plan to deal with. Also, don't lie to yourself thinking you will later get around to reading piles of newsletters. Just unsubscribe; you can re-subscribe when you have more time.

(2) Do Respond to E-mails You Received Yesterday

This trick is called the "Tony Hsieh's Yesterbox technique[3]." You shouldn't be processing e-mails the second they arrive in your inbox. They steal time from you and are always call-

---

[3] http://www.powerlists.org/es86

ing you back to check. Decide that you won't respond to them until the following day. This will slow down your temptation to watch your inbox. In addition, it will lower other people's expectations of how you manage your inbox. Most people don't consider one-day delays to be excessive in replying to e-mail. If something needs handling faster, they should call you.

(3) Do Turn off E-mail Notifications

The last two tricks deal with not constantly checking or handling e-mail. By turning off the pop-up notifications, you reduce the temptation to handle each e-mail upon receipt. I turned off the envelope symbol on my screen and I turned off all pop-up notifications. Thus, the messages aren't visible. Then, I check for new e-mails on my phone every hour, but no more often. A person without the willpower to avoid checking e-mail when seeing an envelope on the screen will still suffer distraction wondering whether or not it is important.

(4) Do Respond to People

When buried under a pile of e-mails, not responding to people can be a serious temptation. Maybe ignoring incoming e-mails is the correct solution. However, ignoring them will create even worse problems. People assume that since they took the time to send you an e-mail, you will read and respond to the e-mail. This doesn't mean you need to do anything more than:

- Read the e-mail.

- Reply, if required.

- Add the e-mail to your task management system.

It will also show that you are an organized and polite person who handles e-mail requests in a timely manner.

(5) Do Unsubscribe to Social Media Notifications

Do you need to see thousands of Facebook or Twitter notifications? You should dedicate a specific time every day when you will check these accounts. Thus, you don't need to receive messages from these services at all. Once you have a routine for checking them daily, you can turn off all e-mail notifications from these services; you'll see a sharp decrease in incoming e-mails.

(6) Do Keep Your E-mails Short

People assume that a long e-mail will be better since it will include a better explanation of what they are trying to convey. However, this is false and the exact opposite is true. The shorter the e-mail, the easier it is for people to process. If they need additional information, they can ask you.

One website went so far as to suggest that you should limit all e-mails to five sentences or less (http://five.sentenc.es/[4]). This is a great way to restrict your temptation to ramble on and on in an e-mail wasting the time of the sender and recipient. In addition, sending brief e-mails will influence the kind and quantity of e-mails you receive.

(7) Do Use Only One Topic per E-mail

Try to confine your e-mail to a single issue. That makes it easier for the person to act upon what you are asking. If I ask someone for help on five issues, they often choose which issues they will address. Many times, they answer the easi-

____

[4]http://www.powerlists.org/7xa9

est questions first and then never return to the harder ones. If there is only one question/task in each e-mail, then they are compelled to answer that issue.

I love it when people follow this strategy with me, sending me separate e-mails for each of the issues they need help with. I register them in my task management system without blurring lines about which project the e-mail is associated with.

(8) Do Use Bullet Points

You should strive for clarity in your e-mail. When you have a list of steps or issues, bullet points are a great solution.

When a person sees your bullet points, they will know what you are communicating. This is useful when you are asking a question. By numbering each question and answer, you save time later when trying to figure out which answer goes with which question.

(9) Do Maintain E-mail Etiquette

Forgetting e-mail etiquette is another common yet avoidable mistake. Many people see e-mail in the same way they see text messages in which you need not say hi or bye – you just write a quick message and forget all of the graces.

This is a terrible idea. It is important to remember that e-mails last forever. You make an impression whenever you meet another person. This includes e-mail. You want to make sure the impression you are giving is good. So, keep your e-mails respectful. You should start with a salutation and finish with a proper closing.

Notice I didn't say you have to be formal. You want to keep common courtesy in place even when shooting off a short e-mail.

(10) Do Avoid Using Negative Emotion in Your E-mail

Any emotion you express in your e-mail is amplified 10 times more than you intended. That means that if your e-mail is sarcastic, it will sound to your reader like extreme aggression. So, don't use e-mail to show negative emotion. It is much better to do that in person.

One exception to this rule is when you express positive

emotions and praise. People should be appreciated and complimented for their work much more often. E-mail is a perfect place to give this recognition. It makes a compliment even more effective, considering it also will be amplified 10 times.

(11) Do Classify Incoming E-mails Into Types

You need to classify incoming e-mails. It is a waste of time to handle all e-mails in the same way. The four basic classifications are e-mails you:

- Could do without

- Need to act on now

- Will take two minutes or less to complete

- Will work on later

The first decision is identifying e-mails you should not have received in the first place. These include spam or irrelevant e-mails. You need to delete them.

Next, you should address the e-mails that demand immediate action. Based upon their priority, you should not delay taking action. Immediate action is also the correct choice when dealing with e-mails that will take two minutes or less to address. The reason for this is that inserting them in your task management system and later retrieving them will take over two minutes. These e-mails may include ones for other people to address. Save yourself time by forwarding them right away.

Insert the e-mails you will address into your task management system and archive them.

(12) Do Use the Search Function to Find Old E-mails

You can use the search function to find e-mails, assuming you are using a good e-mail system that has this functionality. This method works even better when your subject lines contain key phrases that will be easy to retrieve. Sorting different fields in your "by sender" and "sent/received date" allows you to easily find an e-mail.

(13) Do Send E-mails Early or Late in the Day

"People were more responsive when they received e-mails either early in the morning--between 6 and 7--or around 8 at night. At those times, about 40 percent of e-mails received a response." --Erik Sherman at Inc.com[5]

The time of day you send e-mail will affect how long it takes you to get a response. One useful trick can be to put delays on e-mails you send. In Microsoft Outlook and other programs, you can set e-mail to go out at specific times. This does two things for you:

- You will be able to target the most effective periods during the day when people are most likely to respond.

- You slow down the tempo of an e-mail conversation, allowing people to think about the discussion. Quick responses back and forth may prevent proper digestion and consideration of the content.

----

[5]http://www.powerlists.org/pqh0

(14) Do Use Your Subject Fields for Content Summary or a Question

This is one of my favorite tricks. People respond much faster if your e-mail summarizes its content in the subject field. If it is a question, I start the subject field with "Question:" making it clear to the reader that I am asking a single question.

This approach sends them a signal that they can answer this e-mail and delete it. Sometimes this method allows me to get a response ahead of other e-mails in that person's inbox. There is something tempting about responding to an e-mail when you know it will take only a moment.

I appreciate it when others use this trick with me. When I see an e-mail with a clear request in the subject field, I know that I can answer the question quickly. You can give the recipient of an e-mail control and clarity over what to expect when they open an e-mail by starting out with the subject:

- "For info: . . ."

- "Update regarding: . . ."

- "Question: . . ."

- "Important: . . ."

(15) Do Use E-mail to Remember New Tasks

This is one of the most important tricks I have discovered over the years. E-mail can be used as a place to store reminders of new tasks. You can e-mail yourself a message and use the subject field to indicate the task you need to remember.

This method is effective in ensuring you remember important tasks. You take your smart phone out and write a quick note to yourself. I even created a contact on my phone with the letter "Z." Then, whenever I go to the "to" field, I click the letter "Z" to send myself an e-mail. I fill out the subject field with the task/idea I wish to remember and then click send.

Since I started using this method, I haven't forgotten anything unless I forgot to send myself an e-mail.

Although this method isn't related to getting control of your inbox, it is such a good trick I wanted to include it. However, this trick assumes you have control over your inbox and will be able to move this new task to a task management system when you are back at your computer.

(16) Do Use a Spam Filter

Spam is unwanted e-mail you receive without asking for it. Often, spam is someone's marketing effort. People who send spam receive a small fraction of sales of the products they are marketing, but this fraction encourages spammers to continue their efforts.

It is important to have a spam filter. The time you use reading spam isn't free. It is taking away valuable time from other projects. So, install a spam filter on your e-mail. In addition, you can create rules in your inbox to delete specific e-mails from certain senders or to delete e-mails with specific spam text in the subject field.

Another trick spammers use is that they place an unsubscribe button at the bottom of the e-mail. If you read their message and click that button, they learn they have a live person scanning their spam. Instead of unsubscribing, you just subscribed. You also may find yourself on a website that will try to sell you something, making even more money for the spammer. Delete the message without clicking on any links.

(17) Do Give Paragraphs Breathing Room

The use of punctuation makes it easier to see the flow of one idea into the next. Having spaces between paragraphs make it much easier to see when you are finished with an idea and are ready to move onto the next idea.

Reading enormous blocks of text is hard on the eyes and makes it easy to lose your place. This book was written using this method. Limiting each paragraph to a few sentences prevents the reader from getting lost.

(18) Do Use the Out-of-office Response Tool

Another helpful e-mail tool is the out-of-office response. You set your inbox to send an automatic reply when you will be away for the day. This useful tool ensures that people don't expect answers while you are out.

In addition, you can leave a message about who will replace you while you are gone. This will decrease the number of e-mails coming your way. Instead of getting back to your office to discover a pile of unread e-mails, someone else in the office will take care of the issue while you are away.

This trick also may involve giving that other person access to your e-mail account while you are gone. Another option is sharing a common area where all members of the group can read the relevant e-mails.

(19) Do Use Shortcuts for Common Phrases

It is possible in many e-mail programs to set up shortcuts for common phrases. If you type the same phrases over and over, you can set up shortcuts that allow a few key strokes to fill out the rest of a phrase. This saves time.

(20) Do Use a Signature Block

Predefined signatures for your e-mails save you time. It is important that you have a signature at the bottom of all of your e-mails that includes:

- Your full name

- Your title

- Your company

- Your contact information

Even if the person you are e-mailing knows you, future recipients of that e-mail may not be familiar with who you are. So, you save them the time of having to look you up.

Many companies, including my own company, use images in their signature block. This can create problems later when trying to find e-mails with attachments. Those images are stored as attachments and make it impossible to find an e-mail from someone when looking for a response with an attachment since all e-mails from them contain attachments.

A better alternative is to use fonts and color schemes in your signature block that match the company without including a picture.

When people ask for my contact information, I point them to every e-mail I send to them. There should never be a time where you are in dialogue with someone via e-mail without knowing who they are.

(21) Do Change Your Subject Line as the Subject Changes

Just because you start an e-mail with a subject line, doesn't mean that the subject field must stay the same for the entire discussion. After you have written the body of an e-mail, you should consider whether the subject is the same as it was when you first started the correspondence. This is important when an e-mail goes back and forth several times.

You may have received the message with one question or update that switches to a different subject within one or two rounds of correspondence. The subject field is critical when trying to find an e-mail or when deciding later whether to process an e-mail.

(22) Do Follow up on Sent E-mails

This assumption gets many people in big trouble. It is easy

to assume that because you sent an e-mail, you are now free to forget about managing the task behind the request. This is a serious mistake.

A better assumption is to expect that their inbox is overflowing. You need to track whether they respond. I often see this in meetings with people who inadvertently show their inboxes on the projection screen. Their inboxes are filled with thousands of e-mails.

This means they are most likely using their inbox as a task management system. You will need to follow up on any e-mail you send to these people. Never assume that they will get back to you since their inbox is overflowing. The correct choice here may be to meet them as opposed to sending another e-mail.

(23) Do Fill Out the "To:" Field Last

The first item to fill out at the top of your e-mail is the recipient (in the "To" box in the header). Don't start by filling it out. The reason is that it is easy to click the send button before you are finished writing your e-mail. By leaving the "To" box blank until you are ready to send it, the e-mail is prevented from going out until you are ready to send it.

(24) Do Aim for Inbox 0

Inbox 0 is an idea presented at Google several years back that says it is completely possible to maintain an inbox with no e-mails in it. I remember the first time I saw the <u>well-known video</u>[6] on this concept. This video is worth watching. It was rather shocking to hear someone say you could keep an inbox with no e-mails in it. Inbox 0 may seem like a mythical place you might reach if you cut out eating and sleeping.

I believe it is possible to reach this goal. Remember, you are doing a quick sort on each of the tasks in your inbox and not working those issues unless they require 2 minutes or less as discussed earlier. You may be surprised how achievable this goal is. The key is developing habit of properly handling e-mail on a daily basis. For more information on building and breaking habits see my book *Habit Ignition: 41 Steps to Unlocking the Secret Power of Habits and Rituals for Life Book*[7] .

––––––––––––––

[6]http://www.powerlists.org/epo7

(25) Don't Use Folders and Subfolders for Organization

One common way of organizing e-mails is to create subfolders. Storing all e-mails in your inbox is a terrible way of controlling e-mail. The problem is that you have different e-mails for different projects all blended together. You need a solution.

You might have tried to solve this problem by creating subfolders. Under each of those, you continue to create more folders since each project has different relevant e-mails. Some of the folders may be for further reading, or the folders might be organized by sender. Whatever the case, this method is terrible.

The reason it's so bad is that folders take a lot of time to set up and provide little help with all of the work. Like the hydra, cutting off one head means creating more heads. It is much better to create an archive for all of your e-mails and store the header data in your task management system. You can find e-mails by looking up the header data or by run-

---

[7]hthttp://www.powerlists.org/03k6

ning searches on your archive.

(26) Don't Use E-mail as a Task Management System

E-mail doesn't work well as a task management system since it won't remind you when you need to take your next action or when you need to plan particular events. If you want to follow up with someone, it's better to take a copy of the header data from the e-mail. You click reply and then copy the top four lines of e-mail including the following information:

- To

- From

- Date

- Subject

Next, you paste this into another system like Outlook Tasks or any other task system you choose. When it's time to do a task, you can find that e-mail in your archive with the time and date from the header data.

For information about this, check out my book *Achieve Your Goals Now with PowerLists*™[8] .

(27) Don't Double-handle Your E-mail

In the physical world, double-handling is when people move something twice or more. For example, they might pick up a box and move it halfway across the room. Then, later they pick it up again and move it to its final destination. This costs time and money. The correct action is to move the box from its starting point to its final destination at one time. The same principle applies for e-mail. For any given e-mail, you will either read and process it, or you will put it in your task system to handle later. That's it. No other options should be considered. You shouldn't read the e-mail and leave it in your inbox for later. This single trick will help empty your inbox and prevent the double-handling of e-mails.

(28) Don't Respond to E-mails on Your Mobile Devices

There are multiple problems with responding to messages

---

[8]http://www.powerlists.org/xt4x

from your hand-held devices. The main one is that you are much slower at typing on a hand-held device. You will use more time and risk more mistakes. Most likely, you don't have your task management system with you. If you respond or make progress on a project, how can you update your task management system? This creates another double-handling situation.

I understand that it's important to handle important e-mails promptly. Many employers expect you to respond to an issue when you receive it on your phone. However, you should only work issues on your phone in extreme cases. Your phone's purpose is to give you a quick feel for the flow of e-mails but not to handle them.

(29) Don't Constantly Check Your E-mail

"One look at an e-mail can rob you of 15 minutes of focus. One call on your cell phone, one tweet, one instant message can destroy your schedule, forcing you to move meetings, or blow off important things, like love, and friendship." -- Jacqueline Leo

This bad habit is a major time waster. E-mail can take your

focus away from getting something done. The pinging of your phone or the little envelope appearing in the corner of your screen is going to lure you away from your current task. The problem is that this interruption comes with a steep price. The most effective way to work is with chunks of time dedicated to high levels of focus. Too much multi-tasking makes you less effective. So, check your e-mail once every hour. Don't break this rule.

(30) Don't Use Poor E-mail Systems

Although, I won't name them, some e-mail systems are terrible. These include systems with limited storage space. Without enough space, you won't be able to create an e-mail archive you can point to with your task management system.

Other systems or services cannot back up your data properly. This means that a single crash will cause a complete loss of control over your projects. Another problem I have experienced is with a popular system that doesn't allow you to search your e-mails. Since we aren't using thousands of sub-folders, we need to find e-mails later. A search function is key to making this happen. I recommend using G-mail or

Outlook to make sure you have the functionality you need and avoid using alternative programs that create long-term headaches.

(31) Don't Reply to E-mail When Courtesy Copied (CC)

This one gets under my skin. There is no need to include the whole universe in every e-mail we send out. Rather, the "to" field is for the person who needs to do something. Maybe if another person needs a status update on the project, you should CC him or her. However, the overuse of CC results in piles of e-mails that waste everyone's time. In addition, if you receive a message, you might skim it, but don't reply to it since it wasn't to you. People will understand that including you on the CC line means you won't respond to the e-mail. So, skim it and archive it.

(32) Don't Use In-line Answers to E-mails

This is where you ask someone a series of questions and they reply in the text of your e-mail. If you are lucky, they will change the color or font of their answer. This is a terrible practice. It means having to rescan the original e-mail and find what they are answering. I have seen it get even worse when the person getting this response attempts to respond to their responses in the text of the original message and its response. The result is a confusing rainbow soup of text that defies comprehension.

A better choice is to confine the e-mail to a single question or topic. Thus, any response is answering the single issue addressed. If you must restate an issue, copy it to your response and put quotation marks around it.

I will take an e-mail with three questions and respond with three e-mails changing the subject header to match the three different questions. This means when they reply, there is no need to restate what I originally said since I am addressing one issue at a time.

(33) Don't Use E-mail as a Replacement for Meetings

It is tempting to use e-mail as a replacement for a meeting. I am sympathetic to this use of e-mail since many issues can be resolved with a few succinct e-mails.

If you find e-mails bouncing around and never resolving an issue, it is time to call for a meeting or speak to the other person on the phone. I use the rule of two rounds for any given e-mail. I will stop e-mailing at that point if communication is still a problem.

You create a communication barrier when you go two rounds of back and forth e-mails without making progress on an issue. The worst thing you can do is think that e-mails can substitute for a meeting. This complicates the situation even more if additional people are on the CC with everyone replying to all as we go twenty rounds.

(34) Don't Use ALL CAPS AND BOLD!

Writing to someone in all capitalized letters is the same as yelling at them. In the previous trick I told you about how emotion is amplified in e-mail. You should avoid using:

- All caps

- Excessive use of boldface

- Multiple exclamation points

Instead, let your comments be few and express what you are trying to communicate clearly and concisely.

If you want to criticize someone, do it in person. If you are a manager wishing to document issues, write a statement establishing the standard of the company and the actions or behaviors violating that policy. At no point should you add emotion to your e-mails. The temptation is to think that adding emotion will make it more personal. This notion is incorrect.

Use positive emotions. All negative statements toward someone should be factual and devoid of emotion. This ensures that they understand you are serious, but you are not being mean and unfair about the issue.

(35) Don't Use Reply All

Reply all is something you should never do unless you need for everyone to be in on the discussion. Remember that clicking reply all forces everyone on the list to be a part of your comment. They didn't choose to be a recipient and yet they received an e-mail from you. Once a person clicks reply all, the next person will more than likely also click reply all and a pile of e-mails accumulates. It isn't necessary to force people to be a part of a discussion. Only click reply all if it is essential for every person on the list to receive the message.

(36) Don't Send E-mail if You Don't Have to

This trick seems rather simple, but many people don't ask whether they need to send an e-mail. You know how it feels to get an unnecessary e-mail.

Unnecessary e-mail takes your focus away from your work. You also need to make sure you aren't filling up other people's inboxes with e-mails that aren't relevant. By sending out unimportant e-mails, you decrease the attention your important e-mails will get. The basic rule is that you shouldn't send e-mails unless they are necessary.

(37) Don't Click E-mail Links Even When You Know the Sender

Let's say you get an e-mail from your bank telling you to look at your statement or change your password. They include a link to make logging in easy for you. It is a huge mistake to click on that link.

Never click on the link. It is always better to go to the website and look for a message. By moving your mouse over the link, you can see that the hyperlink text doesn't match the bank's webpage address. The goal of the sender is to try to get you to give them your login information so they can steal from you.

Make a habit of never clicking on links in e-mails from official sources. One exception is if the e-mail is from a friend. Failing to start the e-mail with your name or failing to sign their name at the end is an indication their account may have been hacked. Avoid clicking those links as well and instead send an e-mail to them asking if they have a hacked account.

(38) Don't Use E-mail Reset Unless It Is the Last Resort

Resetting your e-mail is not recommended unless your e-mail becomes completely unmanageable. You should think long and hard before doing this since many people will consider it an insult.

As a last resort, you can send a mass e-mail to everyone you know, informing them that your inbox is now overflowing. In addition, tell them you have little chance of answering all of their e-mails and will soon delete them. Ask them to re-send important e-mails.

The techniques mentioned in this book should help you avoid ever having to go to this extreme measure. It is important to remember that all those people spent a lot of time composing their e-mails, and you are now saying that their time was wasted because you mismanaged your inbox.

I have seen this method used once by a manager and it didn't go over well. I still hear from people complaining about this action years later.

5 - Bonus Tips

Here are some addition tips that I have found since the first publication of this book

(Bonus 1) Mark Spam as Spam in Your Inbox

In the past I have previously deleted spam. However, this was a huge mistake. If you mark spam as spam it sends a report to to your e-mail provider that notifies them that whoever sent the e-mail should be blacklisted. This is important since that will decrease the chance that you and other people will receive an e-mail from that sender again. This is a powerful way of reducing the quantity of e-mails in your inbox. If the spam is blocked before it gets to you, you save the time involved in handling it again. In addition, you save other people time as well.

6 - Conclusion

We have now gone through a whole series of tricks and tips on how to manage your inbox and guidelines for sending e-mails. Our goal is to make e-mail the form of communication it could be. It should be an effective way of communicating and processing important information. As long as e-mail is burying us, it has little chance of fulfilling its potential.

I hope you have enjoyed this book. You should now be in a much better position to tame your inbox.

Remember to pick up your *You've Got (Too Much) Mail! Cheat Sheet*[9] if you haven't already downloaded it. It is great as a checklist to see which tricks you have tried and also is a quick one page refresher of the contents of this book.

---

[9]http://www.powerlists.org/2vor

Thank You

As we reach the end of this book, I want to say thanks for reading this book.

Please do me a favor and leave a review here[10] . It only takes a few minutes and makes it possible for others to find this book as well.

If you enjoyed this book, please join my mailing list[11] so I can tell you about new releases, giveaways, and special promotions. I always send out all deals to my subscribers first.

I love hearing from readers so please get in touch via E-mail: chrisabaird@powerslist.org[12]

---

[10] http://www.powerlists.org/9mhm

[11] http://www.powerlists.org/s891

[12] mailto:chrisabaird@powerlists.org

About the Author

Chris A. Baird is the author of the bestselling PowerLists™ book series. Each PowerList™ book is designed to help you get more out of life.

As an expert Data Analyst living in Norway, he researches proven methods for living life more effectively. These topics include:

- Goal Setting

- Habit Building/Breaking

- Exercise

- Travel

- Sleep

- Diet

- E-mail management

Chris has a passion for finding productivity tricks and exploring better ways of working towards goals.

Each of the PowerLists™ books cover specific topics in a list format that is simple to apply to your life immediately.

He earned a Bachelor of Science from the United States Air Force Academy and advanced degrees in Information Resource Management and Human Resource Administration. With decades of experience dealing with complex, simultaneous projects spanning military service as well as management, database development, and analysis in the oil and gas industry, Chris has a way of breaking down complex research and best practices into simple lists.

Chris writes because he is excited about helping people make their goals a reality; he has seen far too many people frittering away their time and money because of unclear goals.

In his spare time, Chris travels around Europe, takes photos, reads, and hikes around Norway with his wife and three children.

Books by Chris A. Baird

98 Best Travel Tips: For Travel Junkies On A Budget With Kids[13]

Easy Sleep Solutions: 74 Best Tips for Better Sleep Health: How to Deal With Sleep Deprivation Issues Without Drugs Book[14]

You've Got (Too Much) Mail! 38 Do's and Don'ts to Tame Your Inbox[15]

Habit Ignition: 41 Steps to Unlocking the Secret Power of Habits and Rituals for Life Book[16]

Achieve Your Goals Now With PowerLists™[17]

---

[13] http://www.powerlists.org/zgfc

[14] http://www.powerlists.org/e080

[15] http://www.powerlists.org/apff

[16] http://www.powerlists.org/03k6

[17] http://www.powerlists.org/xt4x

Disclaimer

This document is geared towards providing exact and reliable information in regards to the topic and issue covered. The publication is sold with the idea that the publisher is not required to render accounting, officially permitted, or otherwise, qualified services. If advice is necessary, legal or professional, a practiced individual in the profession should be ordered.

This information is not presented by a medical practicioner and is for educational and informational purposes only. The content is not intended as a substitute for professional medical advice, diagnosis, or treatment. Always seek the advice of your physician or other qualified health care provider with any questions you may have regarding a medical condition. Never disregard professional medical advice or delay in seeking it because of something you have read.

The information provided herein is stated to be truthful and consistent, in that any liability, in terms of inattention or otherwise, by any usage or abuse of any policies, processes, or directions contained within is the solitary and utter responsibility of the recipient reader. Under no circumstances will any legal responsibility or blame be held against the

DISCLAIMER

publisher for any reparation, damages, or monetary loss due to the information herein, either directly or indirectly.

Last Updated: 25.Aug.2015